I0490704

THE ULTIMATE GUIDE TO USING SOCIAL AND OTHER

PLATFORMS FOR BUSINESSES AND INFLUENCERS

SOCIAL MEDIA

MARKETING

REVAMPED

NICHOLAS DEGOMME

TABLE OF CONTENTS

00

INTRODUCTION

"A man who stops advertising to save money is like a man who stops a clock to save time."
– Henry Ford

SOCIAL MEDIA MARKETING REVAMPED

The internet has been evolving, and so has the age of marketing and social interactions. As you know, the "Social Media Sphere" is taking over the world one day at a time, and its presence is growing at an alarming rate. With every generation getting phones at an earlier age, it's allowing social media and other related fields to expand even faster. With each generation comes a new "smartphone," increasing their knowledge and adaptability with technology.

Let's take it back to the 2000s, where the music was good, fashion was questionable, and social media was almost nonexistent. One of the first social media pioneers paving the way for virtual communication was Friendster. It didn't take long for Friendster to gain popularity, with almost 3 million users by 2008. It wasn't too long after others followed. Wanting to explore what social media had to offer came to MySpace. With its innovative way of sharing photos, music, and a new way of communicating, it's no surprise MySpace gained popularity, pushing Friendster into the metaphorical "deep end" of the social media world. Joining this trend was AOL, who introduced AOL Instant Messenger, making it a powerhouse of mergers and buyouts. Once reaching its peak, AOL, unfortunately, could not keep up and eventually joined Friendster over in the "deep end."

Let's fast-forward a decade or so, and we got ourselves the most prominent and well-known social media platform, that's right— Facebook. Founded on February 4, 2004, by Mark Zuckerberg, Eduardo Saverin, Dustin Moskovitz, and Chris Hughes in a Harvard dorm room, Facebook has rapidly become one of the biggest social networking sites in the world. Within the first year, Facebook accrued over 1 million users—which has since grown exponentially to hit over 2 billion in 2018, and counting.

On November 6, 2017, Facebook shook the marketing world by hosting a convention introducing Facebook Ads. Zuckerberg wanted to connect businesses with their compatible audiences. Facebook Ads can help users learn about new companies, brands, and products. Facebook Ads opened doors for thousands of businesses such as Coca- Cola, and Apple (to name a few).

Businesses realized that having a part in this social media world would allow them to get in touch with their customers and clients directly. Additionally, using social media gives an upper hand to any company that wants to show people what they are really about and how they care for their customers. Using this practice in any business increases their brand's reputation and brings awareness, which will ultimately lead to their longevity.

Now, let's be honest, who doesn't want their business in the back of their customer's mind?

Ten years ago, Google Ads was Google AdWords, and the cost-per-click for any given keyword was next to nothing. Fast-forward to the present day, and now it is extremely difficult to find a keyword that isn't over three or four dollars in a highly competitive industry. Some people are paying over fifty dollars on a click, and rates will keep increasing. That makes it nearly impossible for any new business to get their foot in the door using paid advertising on Google.

Now you're wondering, "Okay, great. Google Ads is expensive; how can I advertise my business now?" Fortunately, there are effective ways to advertise your business without breaking the bank explained in this book!

Which is the best one for your business? There are so many to choose from, and you can pick them all!

Social media platforms are so important now that they play an enormous role with Search Engine

Optimization (SEO). Check this out, if you have a Facebook page, go search your organization's name on Google and chances are you'll see your Facebook page right on top of the search results. This shows you how powerful social media platforms can be for your brand's reputation. It takes 60 seconds to make a good impression; in this case, it takes one click. Like most Facebook users, your customers will most likely go through your page to see what you stand for. It's crucial in the social media world to make an everlasting impression.

Here's a question: what is the one thing people can't stop looking at? If they need entertainment, where do they turn to by default? Their phones. Most people nowadays are glued to their phones, and the majority are on social media. In 2019, mobile devices surpassed TVs as being the most used device, so you can see how important social media is to your business.

Last question: when you see a sporting event that millions of people watch, what do you suspect as the reason prominent brands place their logos over critical spots? There's only one answer, brand awareness.

Brand awareness plays a huge factor when it comes to reaching the masses. As a business owner, having a steady clientele is the main goal, and branding will play a significant role in your digital marketing efforts. Big brands use this simple yet effective form of advertising technique to attract millions of new potential customers. What if I told you that your business, no matter what state it's currently in, can use an identical tactic without spending a fraction of what these big brands pay?

The method many expanding companies use to reach their targeted audience is by using social media advertising.

For example, companies that use Facebook Ads, and are implementing videos as their ads will pay cents to get their business seen by thousands of users on this platform. That's 2 billion people you could potentially be showing your ads to, and the exposure is far more powerful than a TV ad. Social media marketing keeps your advertising budget low and even allows you to target your exact audience for an extremely affordable cost-per-click compared to search engine marketing (Google and Microsoft Ads).

In this book, you will learn many new methods that will elevate your knowledge about digital marketing. Not only will you gain marketing insights, but you will also have access to different tactics for social media marketing that will generate massive profit while attracting a new audience.

Computers, cellphones, and tablets have completely revolutionized the way businesses engage with their audience.

In this book you will find out the short and simple way to use social media to your advantage.

01

WHICH SOCIAL

PLATFORMS

SHOULD A

BUSINESS BE

ON

*"Automation is going to cause unemployment, and we
need to prepare for it."*
- Mark Cuban

In the modern era, we can hardly find a reputable business organization without any social platform relevancy. Many businesses before this time of the social rush could get by with the simple e-mail marketing campaign or the old-fashioned cold calling (which can still be used but is not nearly effective as the use of social media if done correctly). With this being said, here are the top social media platforms that any business should dive into to stay up to date and not become a dinosaur.

Instagram

Of course, our first pick would be Instagram. One of, if not the most, popular social media platforms of our time. It is the leading cause of success for many businesses, reaching audiences all over the world itching for that new product or service they've been waiting for. If your business is not utilizing Instagram already, chances are you're not reaching your primary audience. With the power of photos and videos, reaching your target audience will be accomplished.

Since September 2017, Instagram has reached almost 1 billion active users; that number should be an automatic trigger in your brain, telling you that you need to harness this platform for your business. Mobilizing this massive network and the potential to reach thousands and/or millions of potential customers will elevate your business to another level. In 2015, there were more than 77.6 million active Instagram users in the United States. This figure is projected to surpass 111 million in 2019. Here are some key insights that you need to know for your business:

- *1 billion people use Instagram.*
- *80% of users are not from the United States.*

- *77.6 million Instagram users are from the United States. Instagram's Mobile Ad revenue is expected to hit $10 billion in 2022.*
- *There is a ratio of 39% Women & 30% Men using the application.*
- *59% of users are below age 30.*
- *72% of teens use Instagram every day!*
- *72% of users have purchased a product on Instagram.*

I can go on and on about facts that will show you how vital it is to tap into this platform. Make sure you know what you are doing when you start advertising on anything. Read this book, hire an agency, search the web, listen to some podcasts, or join a class. Not doing this will result in a lot of trial and error, as well as money down the drain.

Using multiple social platforms can give you ultimate reach.

Facebook

This platform did probably the smartest business move of this era. Facebook bought out Instagram on April 9, 2012, for 1 billion dollars. This move was obviously made by the social media powerhouse due to Instagram getting a massive boost in popularity, making it a major competitor. Facebook is by far in the top three most-used social platforms, and that is why we ranked it second on our list. Also, it is one of the cheapest ways to get your business out there!

This is ideal for small to medium-sized businesses with limited marketing budgets. However, larger companies can fully utilize this with marketing concepts and different campaign themes through Facebook before committing to bigger advertising plans.

Other than posting the text of your next business venture or just trying to get to know your audience, Facebook lets you upload pictures and videos from your business, like Instagram. This can be a powerful way to communicate with customers and clients, allowing them to have a preview of a product or service without having to visit your organization. Nowadays, people don't even have to leave their house to go shopping. Thanks to social platforms, business deals can be done in the comfort of your own home.

Additionally, Facebook uses algorithms that analyze detailed information that millions of users enter into their profiles or search engines. As the owner of a business page, you can pay a certain price to utilize this key information to deliver targeted advertising to a specific group. For example, a shoe store could use Facebook to calculate how many women over a certain age in a specific city have listed 'shoes' as an interest. Then they could develop an ad for a newly trending shoe and pay for it to appear only on the pages of those people. This is a very powerful tool that your business needs to harness. The targeting options are almost endless and can be a bit overwhelming. Make sure you are not spending money on the wrong people.

YouTube

YouTube is a video-focused social media network that continues to have a growing audience. This social platform is number three on our list.

Launched in 2005, YouTube is web and mobile-based with over 1 billion active users. Google bought the platform in November 2016, which is why YouTube accounts are linked to Google accounts. Just like Facebook and Instagram, YouTube has similar ways you can engage your audience, such as:

Subscriptions: The best way for users to stay up to date with your brand's content is to subscribe. Every time a user uploads a new video, a subscriber will receive a push notification. Easily the most important topic on this list, you should continuously encourage your viewers to subscribe, this will enhance engagement in the long run and boost the longevity of your channel.

Comments: Comments can be organized by "most popular" or "new" and can even be deleted. Engaging with users who comment on your videos boosts the video's engagement traffic. This is a great way to get your brand name out there. However, it can be time-consuming.

Likes: This is a more passive form of interacting with content, with minimal impact. However, if you've chosen to show your likes publicly on your channel, the videos you like will appear as a playlist on your page.

Playlists: Organize the proper content using the site's playlist feature. If you choose to publicize them, playlists will appear on your channel's page below your uploaded content. This is a way to organize your content on your channel.

Sharing: The site's social widget allows users to share videos on other social media networks, such as Instagram, Facebook, Twitter, Pinterest, Reddit, Tumblr, and LinkedIn.

AD OPTIONS

There are four video ad options:

TrueView: TrueView in-stream ads play before, during, or after other videos (the yellow line on the video duration marker). After 5 seconds of these ads, users can skip the ad. You'll only be charged for the ad when a viewer watches 30 seconds of the video or interacts with the video, which is an excellent way for the engaged audience to see a great preview of your business.

Posting on YouTube will build an excellent image for your brand by speaking directly to your audience.

Discovery Ads: Discovery Ads appear when a user is searching or browsing content on YouTube or across the web. These clips aren't limited to 30 seconds, and they can be as short or as long as you intend them to be.

Bumper Ads: Bumper Ads are 6 seconds or less, and users can't skip these. These ads also appear before, during, or after another video.

Out Stream: Out Stream ads can only play on mobile devices, on partner websites, and within other apps. You'll be charged for these ads based on cost per thousand impressions (CPM).

Twitter

"Twitter is where people come to discover what's happening." Catchy and partly true, like most social platforms, Twitter is a place that users use pictures and text to engage their audience. Boasting over 500 million tweets being sent each day, hundreds of millions of people exploring links, articles, retweets, and trends, this is a place to learn where the market is going.

There are six parts to a Twitter profile – a Twitter handle, a profile picture, a username, biography, header image, and pinned tweet. This is the foundation of your business on your account; this shows people what you have in store for them right off the bat.

Your Twitter handle is your "@name" and is your identifier. It can have up to 15 characters and should symbolically represent your business. Your profile picture should visually represent your business and brand, as well. Make it right, as every tweet you make will have your profile image and name, so keep that in mind.

For your biography, you have 160 characters to describe who you are as a business. Try to include information such as your location, business hours, and a link to your website. Introduce your brand and what you are made of; this is a huge factor in bringing in new clientele. The header image behind your profile picture can be used to highlight specific things like promotions, giveaways, events, or news.

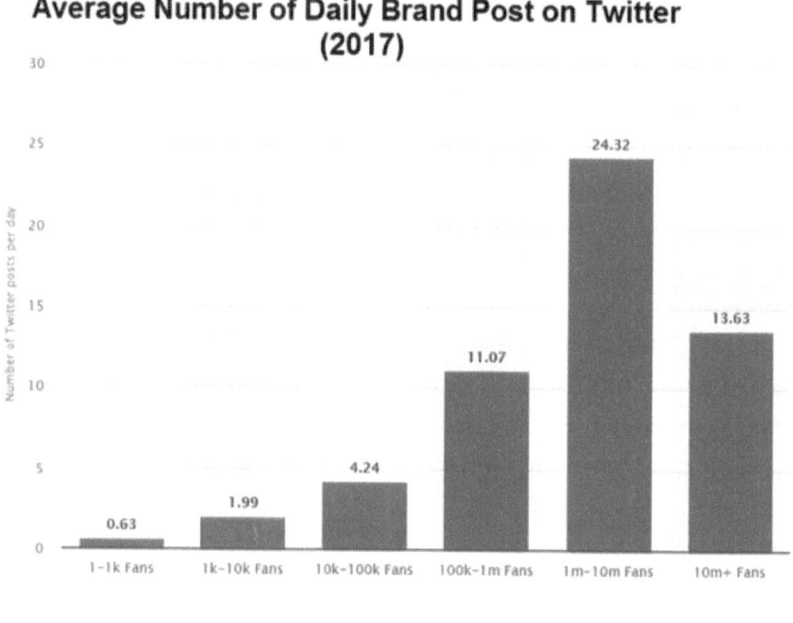

Average Number of Daily Brand Post on Twitter (2017)

Twitter allows for your business to stay on trends.

Lastly, your pinned tweet is the first tweet people see when they visit your profile. Just like your biography, it can also be a significant factor in your Twitter image/presence. Like Facebook and Instagram, you can always go back to it if you are not satisfied and change it.

Twitter uses the same principles to target your primary clientele, by using hashtag targeting, engaging photos, creative text, polls for people to engage on, and many more to get your business relevant on this social platform.

LinkedIn

With more than 560 million users, LinkedIn is one of the most powerful social media platforms on the internet. It's one of the best platforms for business-to-business (B2B) marketers to advertise on.

Just like most of the platforms we touched on, LinkedIn gathers information about its users, such as occupation, position, skills, etc. Advertising is relativity the same in regards to the targeting formats the platform has to offer.

Capabilities that allow you to use filters like industry, company size and job title to target specific types of individuals. Using this information will direct you to your target audience.

Being one of the greatest hubs to meet professionals, we have never had the opportunity to speak with high-level experts so easily as we do on LinkedIn.

One of the unique tools LinkedIn offers is the capability to have pre-filled texts automated for your target audience. You can use sponsored "In-Mail" or "Direct Messaging" to speak directly to users who match your specific criteria.

You can also use text ads, which can run on a pay-per-click (PPC) or a cost-per-impression (CPM) model. This works similar to using Google Ads or Microsoft Ads, which is something that we will touch on later in this book. These ads allow you to increase the visibility and relevancy of your company and will potentially lead to more business if done right.

This is a win/win for both business owners and users. Business owners who do their marketing have access to lead data that is accurate and high quality, and users don't have to spend time filling out the contact forms.

Amazon

Not quite a social media platform, we need to touch on Amazon as a platform of choice. If you're in the product selling industry, this is your "pot of gold." One of the leading online retailers — Amazon. If you are not selling products, then you can skip this.

Using Amazon as an online platform to sell your product will be a GAME CHANGER for your business! It is not quite a social platform, however it has social aspects like product reviews, which little do people know, can be a perfect way to advertise your company.

Incorporating as much human interaction as possible during your customer's purchase on Amazon can lead to better brand recognition. For example, in your product description, make sure you emphasize that your customer can ask you any question they want about the product. Even reviewing similar products from other companies can lead to brand awareness.

Having Amazon as an outlet for your customers to shop is more of a convenience. Most people tend to shop on Amazon for all their online shopping needs.

02

HOW TO USE

PAY-PER-CLICK

ADVERTISING

" Dreamers and Doers are not two different types of people. All the best entrepreneurs are a bit of both. "
-Mandy McEwen

Chances are your business is utilizing pay-per-click in a search or social platform already; if not, you need to start now. PPC is the modern-day Yellow Pages with a greater reach. Many popular search engines and social platforms use this for businesses to get in touch with their targeted audience. Listed below are some of the companies many companies use and what we specialize in:

- **Google Ads:** Google is by far the most-used search engine and PPC ad platform option. It allows companies and advertisers to research optimal keywords, however they are the most expensive.

- **Microsoft Ads:** As the second-most-used search engine, Microsoft Ads typically cost less than Google Ads and appear on many search engines such as Yahoo. We recommend using Microsoft Ads because it translates to 1/3 of business for many businesses.

- **Facebook:** One of the cost-effective forms of PPC, Facebook is by far the most used and is commonly coupled with Instagram. Our favorite choice of advertising.

- **Amazon:** Amazon is the largest online retail company in the world. With revenues continuing to soar, any business needs to put its product on this platform to maximize revenue.

- **Instagram:** Whether your business is big or small, using this platform will provide social proof to your clientele. Creating visually appealing images as a means of putting forth an important message, Instagram may be an excellent platform for your PPC campaign.

Write or type which platform you will use on your notes
and try to experiment with each one.

Managing Pay-Per-Click Costs

Knowing your business goal(s) is key. Some things to ask yourself are:How much revenue or profit are you looking to obtain each month? If you're a lead-based business, how many qualified leads are you looking to have, and what is their average value? Knowing the answer to these questions will be the foundation for your PPC goals.

Here's an example: Andres owns a retail business and wants to do $100k in sales per month from PPC and turn a profit. The average value per transaction is $75, and the profit margin on his products is 40%, meaning he makes $30 in profit per transaction. This means the maximum amount he can spend in PPC per month to drive $100k in revenue is around $40,000. Going over this targeted number will result in a loss in profit.

Continuing Andres's goal, he wants to drive $100k in revenue from PPC and make $10,000 in profit. This means his maximum budget is $30,000, and his minimum Return on Ad Spend (ROAS) is 333%.

Max. Budget = ($100k Revenue x 40% Profit Margin) – $10k Profit = $30,000

Min. ROAS = $100k Revenue / $30k Cost = 333%

Now that Andres knows his target budget per month, he can use an estimated conversion rate, let's say 4%, to determine how many clicks it will take to generate that revenue and what the average cost per click (CPC) needs to be to accomplish his profit target:

Est. Transactions = $100k Revenue / $75 Avg. Value = 1,334 (rounded up)

Est. Conversion Rate (CVR) = 4%

Est. Clicks = 1,334 Transactions / 4% CVR = 33,350

Max. Avg. CPC = $30k Cost / 33,350 Clicks = $0.90

Andres now knows that he'll need to obtain more than 33,000 clicks at an average of $0.90 per click from a $30,000 PPC budget to acquire his desired revenue and profit target. If the actual conversion rate ends up being better than 4%, he can bid a bit higher to go after more traffic and more revenue and still meet his desired profit target.

If it does not turn out how he anticipated, he'll need to decrease bids to save on click costs and evaluate if there's enough potential traffic to generate the number of clicks necessary to meet his revenue and profit goals.

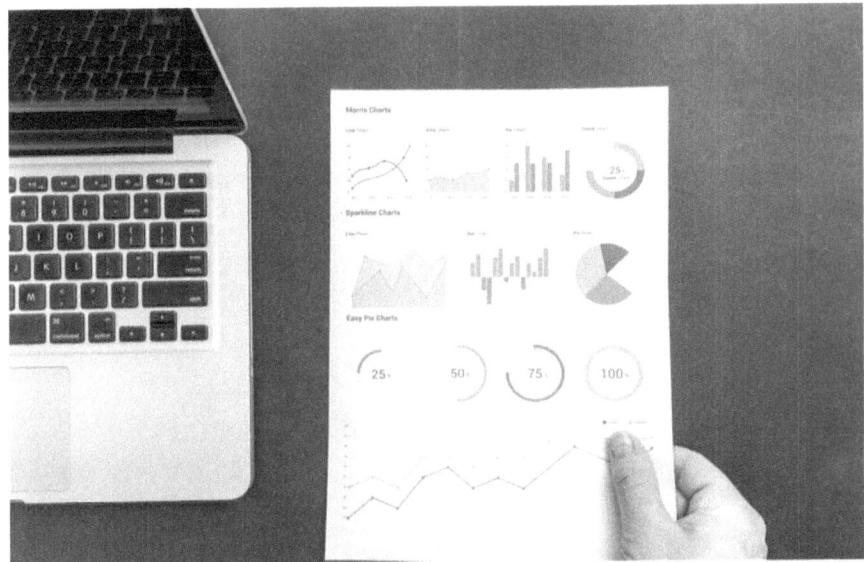

Understanding the basics of Google Ads is all you need to
do to tap into a whole other audience.

Re-Targeting & Asking the Right PPC Questions

Re-marketing ads are shown to people who have visited your business's
website or mobile app in the past. These ads can help you reach visitors
who have expressed interest in your products or services and can help
to encourage conversions. Most of the time, people need to see ads up-
wards from two to three times to convert.

These ads can be shown on the Display Network or as Search Ads. The
platforms that support this immensely are search engines such as Google
and Bing, even social media platforms. There are steps to set up campaigns; however, it may be worth the increased click-through and conversion rates to narrow your ad audience to those who have already
made a connection with your business.

Setting up your re-targeting campaign the right way will allow you to
get those indecisive customers. There are many times when you

searched for "that shoe" you have been wanting, but you have been putting it off. There is a huge chance that when you visited that site, they were trying to target you again after your experience.

With a clearer understanding of how PPC works, your next step should be to ask yourself a few questions: How does PPC advertising work for my organization in the context of my overall marketing campaign? To answer this, ask yourself:

"What goals am I hoping to achieve through PPC?"

"How does my industry/competition typically use PPC?"

"What is the budget?"

"How does this compare to my goals and my competitor's budgets?"

"Does the company have the capabilities to manage my campaigns actively on a regular basis?"

"How else am I building a relevant, highly visible, high-converting online presence through social media networks like Instagram or Facebook?"

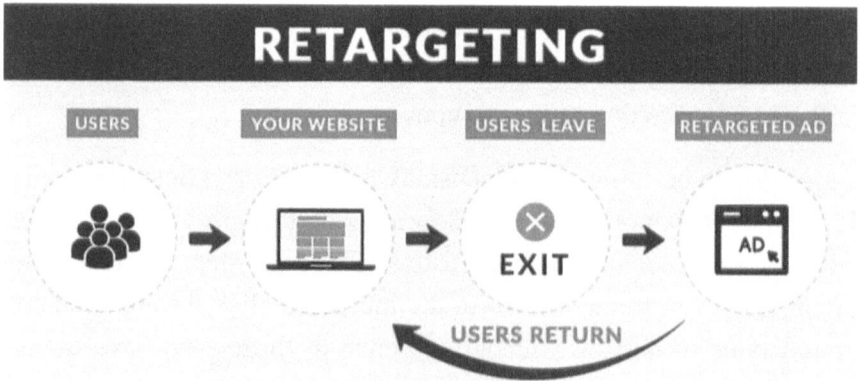

Re-targeting will be a huge factor in gaining clients or customers, double down on it.

03

EFFECTIVELY

ADVERTISING

YOUR BUSINESS

> *"Starting and growing a business is as much about the inno-*
> *vation, drive, and determination of the people behind it as the*
> *product they sell."*
> **- Elon Musk**

In the last chapter, we touched on "Business Goals," and with every new year, comes a new goal for your business. One goal many businesses have in common is to drive more sales by attracting more customers;this is all easier said than done. In this chapter we will be discussing the proven ways that got many of our clients on the right track into attracting more people to their businesses.

Social Media & Social Proof for Business Growth

Many companies in the past have done fine without the help of social media, generating outstanding numbers only with the help of search engine advertising such as Google, Microsoft, and Yahoo Ads. The way modern consumers are drastically shifting their minds on whether or not to buy a product or service is by using social media.

Let's face it, we catch ourselves glued to our phones throughout the day, and we happen to scroll across engaging ads on Facebook or Instagram. Here's an example, a customer notices an ad that catches their attention, which has many comments and many likes, so they click to see what it is all about. When customers arrive at the page, they'll see captivating content that catches their eye and carry on browsing posts with amazement. Eventually, the customer will stop and think, "I'm not sure if this is legit," (which we're all guilty of). When that happens, that customer will instinctively try to find out whether anyone else has liked or reviewed this product or service.

You can see where I'm headed with this. Many people nowadays require social proof to act on a purchase. Whether it is looking through Yelp to find a restaurant, going on Instagram to see when the store is having a sale, or see how many reviews an Amazon product has, this all plays a huge factor in this decision process. Here we highlight some insights on social media consumer habits:

- *People tend to spend 31% more when a company has excellent ratings and reviews.*
- *72% of online shoppers trust consumer opinions online.*
- *90% of buyers report being influenced by online reviews.*
- *75% of all people are rationalizers, which means they're looking for unbiased facts and opinions to help them make their decision.*

Having a happy customer will lead you to many more.
Plain and simple.

Experiences Count

Our society is moving from a more product-based economy to a service-based one, with an increased focus on the experiences received during the visit. As people spend more money on doing things rather than buying them, the retail experience must stay relevant to stay ahead. When someone goes into a store, they want the ultimate experience, such as premium customer service, exceptional décor (especially photo opportunities for their social media), and the last thing should be the product(s) you introduce.

Successful businesses will listen to their customers to find out what will meet their needs and make them feel special. You can randomly select customers that venture into your organization and survey them as to what can improve your business. If you have regulars, then they would be a prime target.

Recognizing that not everyone will be drawn to your business with the "next best thing" always lurking in ads, it's imperative that the customer experience is well... an experience. The future of the physical organization is not about purchase transactions. It's about cultivating experiences, events, and brand associations, which helps create memories, and most importantly, loyalty for that customer or client.

Leveraging Amazon for Your Business

One of the biggest reasons why brick-and-mortar stores are going out of business is due to the easy access of having a "store" in the palm of your hand, especially with a company as big as Amazon. Most people will do whatever they can to compete with this retail behemoth, but chances are their margins are not doing as great as they should be.

While Amazon has fees and a tedious starting process, it is well worth it. The giant online retail store has millions of users that engage on their site religiously. Take advantage of this opportunity and put your products on the site. It is a very competitive space, and chances are a numerous amount of companies are selling the same product.

Have no fear, with the right approach; you can get ahead of your competitors and start selling in no time. It is a time-consuming process, but having a great team will assure success. However, if you want to take on this task alone, head your way to over to Amazon Seller and make an account!

Customer Loyalty

Offering a loyalty program and implementing special deals cannot only be beneficial to bringing in new clientele, but it also maintains your loyal customers. Keeping a loyal customer base can be profitable in the growth of your business.

This steady flow of income is a positive reinforcement and brings a loyal presence to your business. Incentives such as discounts on the next meal, referral coupons, happy hours, and meal vouchers upon bringing a plus-one can increase your restaurant's customer feedback and growth exponentially.

A critical side tip that can increase not only your customer count but also a massive potential audience is to promote your business globally. Targeting prospective tourists that will be going to your region, or tourists that are already in the area, are perfect strategies to get your business name out there.

Always greet your customers whenever you have
the chance. Even online.

Being a Local Business Icon

Having a local presence is essential; you could impact the community in a great way. Work with your community in the same way that brick-and-mortar stores do to generate interest and loyalty (just like the loyalty program we went over).

Consider sponsoring local youth sports, having your team participate in 5Ks, volunteering, taking out ads in the local paper or local magazines, and spending some of your digital advertising budget targeting local searches from customers. Local SEO (Search Engine Optimization) can enhance your overall SEO endeavors while furthering your community engagement.

The goodwill that local stores can create by being a part of the local community is available to e-commerce brands as well, but unfortunately, many pass up the opportunity and miss out on its benefits. Use your location as a beacon for your brand; allow your presence to make a more significant impact on the surrounding area.

Make your physical or online store presence a memorable
one to your customer.

Imitate Your Favorite Store

We all have stores we love to go to, even to be inside without making a purchase. Take a minute to think of the store you most enjoy entering. List a few key factors on why you love this store and what brings you back to it. Questions like: Do they know your name and what you always order? Are you met with a friendly greeting every time you walk in? Do they always have your size available? Do you only have to talk to people when you want to? Is everything organized? Do they always have what you want? This list can go on and on.

Take this list of things you like and find out to see if your customers like them too. It should give you some significant insight into how your visions are reflecting on your audience. Sometimes we think our service, offers, and environment are on point to what we want, but chances are your customers beg to differ. Accommodate them as much as possible; sometimes you need to let go of old traditions and adapt to new ones.

Even if these don't work for your customers, the process will have you thinking about ways to improve your business. It is the perfect beginning to the consistent brainstorming that any successful business requires in order to thrive in the short and long term. Search more ways to keep your business ahead here.

04

THE ROAD TO

BECOMING AN

INFLUENCER

*"The people who are crazy enough to think they can
change the world are the ones that do."*
- Steve Jobs

An influencer on social media is a person who has built a reputation for their knowledge and expertise in a particular field of interest (travel, style, food, etc.). They regularly post about their field on their preferred social media channels and generate large followings of loyal and engaged people who pay close attention to their actions.

Brands love social media influencers because they can create trends and encourage their followers to buy products they promote. Many brands have used this tactic of recruiting influencers to increase their sales and brand awareness exponentially. The time is now to become an influencer or use one, while social media is rapidly growing every single day.

Types of Influencers

Most influencers fit into the following categories, with the last category by far is the most attainable and most important today:

- *Celebrities*
- *Industry Experts*
- *Thought Leaders*
- *Bloggers and Content Creators*
- *Micro-Influencers*

The majority of social influencer marketing today occurs in social media, primarily on Instagram, and predominantly with micro-influencers, and blogging. Micro-influencers are often the most informed in their specialties. They have an engaged community of followers who rely on them and trust the content they bring out. They are believable and credible because they are usually everyday people sharing their passion, their recommendations, and their daily life. That is why micro-influencers are important; because they can relate to the ordinary person, which is why brands use them to promote their products.

Industry experts and thought leaders, like journalists, can also be considered influencers and hold an important position for brands. Then there are celebrities. Celebrities were the original influencers of our era. This type of influencer is, unfortunately, not in reach for many people, and brands need to fork up a big price to use a celebrity as an influencer. Influencers and bloggers on social media have the most authentic and active relationships with their fans. Brands are now recognizing and encouraging this with their growth plans. Find out which social platform is better suited for you here.

Some elite influencers get more than $100k a post to sponsor a product.

What Type of Influencer Do You Want to Be?

To become an Instagram influencer, the first thing you need to do is find "That Thing" that will draw people in. It needs to be something you're passionate about, and something in which you have a good deal of knowledge and interest.

Picking something you're passionate about lets future clientele know that you know what you're talking about. Trust me, in this day and age, people WILL take notice and will not hesitate to call you out. Maybe you love to travel and want to talk about it, or perhaps you love food and have a great deal of interest in different types of cuisines, perhaps you're into fashion and are always aware of the latest styles and trends. Your Instagram posts should reflect the image you are trying to portray. Take high-quality photos that engage your audience and allow for new ones to be interested.

Your forte might even be a combination of different things, as long as they're not random. Here's an example of an Instagram influencer whose interest is mostly soccer, but incorporates lifestyle and style itself.

Pick what you love as an influencer, build a strategy, and the rest will follow.

Create an Interesting Biography

Once you have decided on the field of interest, your page will consist of; you need to start working on the details of your social media account. The first thing that you need to focus on is creating a Biography (Bio) that immediately catches people's attention. Your Bio should express who you are and what your business is about to engage anyone (most importantly your potential clientele/audience). Keep in mind; it's one of the first things that a brand or a potential follower sees on your account. So, if you want to become an Instagram influencer make it noteworthy and memorable.

Make a Habit of Posting Consistently

Consistently posting your content is another crucial prerequisite to becoming a social media influencer. Most influencers on Instagram post daily or every other day. However, some of them post a few times a day or even a few times a week. It really depends on your goal as an influencer. Make sure to not bombard your followers with posts that do not intrigue them, as this will lead to unfollowing due to your account becoming repetitious or an overload of "promoting." You need to have a healthy balance of different alternatives when bringing out your content.

Studies have revealed that an increase in your content posting frequency can boost engagement rates. When you decide what your posting schedule needs to be, make sure that you choose wisely. Hiring a Social Media Manager will aid in this process and can dramatically boost your overall performance. Having a Social Media Manager allows you to create your content in advance and set the dates and times for posting, so you don't need to do it yourself. Leave the work to them and allow their expertise to guide you to becoming a prominent influencer.

A perfect example of an engaging bio that additionally describes the page and what it has to offer.

Making an Instagram Business Account

Besides having a catchy Bio, making your account a business page is vital to your success as an influencer. Having your page as a business allows you to view key insights for the development of your social media account. Here is what a business account on Instagram does:

Insights: The most crucial benefit is that with a business account, you get access to insights.

You'll be able to see not only your follower demographics but also which posts are getting better engagement, as well as which days and times your follower engagement is at its peak. This is great information to tap into!

Follower Demographics: Follower demographics are very useful when it comes to pitching to other businesses when interested in collaborating. Since numbers do not lie, showing what numbers your business pulls and from what areas will be key factors to promote your partner's product as well.

Ads: The other advantage you get with a business account is the ability to run ads. You can promote one of your posts in order to get some additional engagement, but for a cost. Social media ads are definitely one of the cheaper avenues of trying to promote a product or business and can be utilized by many classes of influencers.

Using Story Posts

Instagram Stories and IGTV are receiving the biggest hype right now on Instagram; more and more users are joining this bandwagon. In fact, more than 200 million Instagram users are using them every day. This makes Insta Stories and IGTV outstanding tools to grow more followers and gain better visibility. Even utilizing IGTV (which works a bit like YouTube) will be a massive factor for your engagement with your clientele/audience.It helps establish a relationship because you can interact with them via these channels.

Build deeper connections with your clientele/audience by using Insta Stories and IGTV. It will give you a huge advantage as an influencer/business owner.

Even people who aren't your followers can discover you from Insta Stories or IGTV. By adding hashtags or location to your stories, you can be found by more people. An important tip for experienced influencers is that if you have 10,000+ followers, you can include a link using a "swipe up" option on Insta Stories. After you've reached this level, you know you have a considerable advantage over many influencers out there.

You can even tag others on your Insta Stories and give shout-outs to other accounts. This is not only a great way of building relationships with fellow influencers; it can increase your follower count without spending a penny.

Putting these tips into practice can help increase your social media account. The road to becoming an influencer is one that requires patience, persistence, and dedication to sit with the best. Don't be "that person" who buys all their followers and has little to no engagement, things like that don't go unnoticed. Work hard, and your goals will be met, I assure you of that.

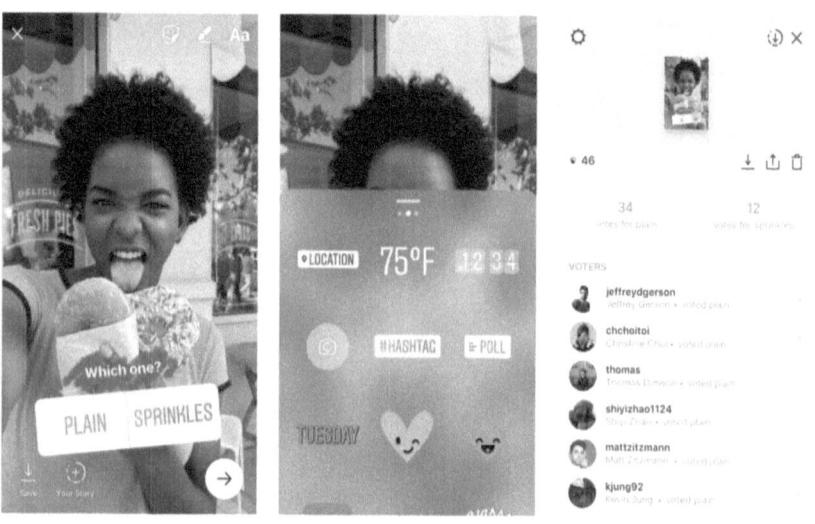

Be you and the right audience will start coming, and new opportunities will present themselves. There will be critics, but it is all part of the process of becoming a successful influencer.

05

GETTING

SPONSORED

AS AN

INFLUENCER

"There is a powerful driving force inside every human being that once unleashed can make any vision, dream, or desire a reality."
- Tony Robbins

Nowadays, everyone wants to be relevant in the social media universe. Whether it's with a massive following or just trying to appeal to the masses, all potential influencers want one thing—sponsorship. Many people nowadays can indeed be titled an influencer; however, not many people can be successful at it. If you are reading this chapter, chances are you will establish the rank of a "micro-influencer," which is a great accomplishment due to the vital role these influencers play in the social media industry. Below are some key points to learning just how to get sponsored by brands and become an influencer.

Who is a Micro-Influencer?

The majority of social media influencers today reside on Instagram and predominantly with micro-influencers and bloggers. Micro-influencers are often very knowledgeable in their niche. They have an engaged community of followers who rely on and trust the content they bring out.They are believable and credible because they are usually everyday people sharing their passion, their recommendations, their everyday life, and their likes and dislikes. This is why micro-influencers are very important. They can relate to the everyday person, which is why businesses use them to promote their products.

Become a huge influence in a small community.

Image Is Vital!

Influencers become popular because people relate to their specific interests and value their opinions tremendously. The idea is that an influential Instagram account focuses on a particular field and does an excellent job of portraying different aspects, and their expertise on it.

As far as what an influencer is specifically known for, it may be the kinds of photos they post, such as a traveling page, which only associates with nature, photography, vacation, etc. Depending on what you want to specialize in, you can venture off or branch into similar niches, which will, in turn, get you a better chance of landing a sponsorship. For example, travel influencers can start doing motivational quotes and start reviewing books to attract authors, magazines, or apps that can relate to their page.

Influencers gain trust from their followers because these followers see them as "experts" in that field. As a result, businesses like working with influencers because they make it easier for their products to reach a specific clientele/audience.

If you want to get serious and start getting sponsored on Instagram, start by thoroughly defining your brand. This can be a gradual process and can take some trial and error, so test things out and see what works best for you. Some people know what they want exactly; if that is the case, make sure to stick with it and perfect it. With that being said, don't be afraid to experiment as well, with different types of content like unique images and videos on your Instagram, and Insta Stories.

How will you be perceived by your audience? Choose wisely; they watch your every move.

Bonus: A successful tactic you can use when you are posting is to tag businesses. When you feature content with products from a business, you like to tag their Instagram page so that when they like your post it will be discoverable to their followers, if they like your posts enough, they will re-post your content on their page, which also gives you exposure to their followers.

It's important to note that when you do this, you are aware of the quality of the images you're tagging businesses in. These images and your feed as a whole, act as a portfolio of the future work you will produce for them. Put out the best content, and surely the right business will come to you.

parkeryorksmith • Follow
Hollywood Walk of Fame

parkeryorksmith I let my socks handle my greetings. | When I heard that my friends at @hotsox had teamed up with the people at @artproductionfund, I had to get involved. || You can grab these and 3 other limited edition socks at @barneysny || #sponsored #APFSox

parkeryorksmith @kylebennettdavid for sure thank you buddy

parkeryorksmith @alexsalceco haha thanks a lot dude

parkeryorksmith @simplealexz cool thanks a lot

parkeryorksmith @fashion4men0 awesome thank you so much

icontrendy Nice socks

corrado_firera Super cool shot bro 😊 ^

♡ ○　　　　　　　　　　🔖

1,095 likes

We tell our clients to pick an influencer role model and try to take some key attributes from them.

06

WHY YOUR

BUSINESS

SHOULD SELL

ON AMAZON

> *"Chase the vision, not the money. The money will end up following you."*
> ### - Tony Hsieh

If you haven't noticed by now, the online retail market is dominated by Amazon. This behemoth of an e-commerce company had nearly $178 billion (USD) net sales by 2017, which, according to "Statista," is a big jump from the $42 billion they made in 2016 — convinced yet? Amazon Marketplace is crucial to a business. In this chapter, we'll be sharing some insights to help jump-start your new (or revamped) business journey.

The Basics of the Amazon Marketplace

Selling your products on Amazon is as easy as 1,2,3. If you're like most people who work the 9 AM-5 PM, starting a "side hustle" that could potentially become your full-time job is exciting but at the same time, petrifying. Using Amazon's Fulfillment by Amazon (FBA) plan can help ease that fear and save some money.

By using the FBA business program, you'll be able to delegate logistical tasks such as sorting products in fulfillment centers, packing and shipping orders, and customer service inquiries. There will be some fees, but the convenience is priceless. Listing yourself as an "individual" through the FBA will have a small percentage deducted per sale (as well as other fees), but you won't have the full benefit of someone who's listed as a "professional." Being listed as a "professional" is a fair $39.99 (other fees not included); however, the satisfaction of knowing your business is logistically being taken care of by a company like Amazon is gratifying.

How much the FBA program will cost you depends on your product's size and weight along with the type of FBA services you use. What you can expect to pay is 6-20% of your sales, with 15% being the typical amount the retailer takes. Make sure you pick the right product(s) to sell and/or know-how to advertise the right way by taking advantage of social media.

There are other benefits to consider with the FBA program. Amazon Prime members can pay for products without being charged extra in shipping fees, and eventually, you can qualify to have your account badged as an FBA seller without even using Amazon's warehouses! Just know this tip, having that badge will make your products more attractive to customers and bring absolute opposition to those businesses who aren't in the FBA program.

Sales Summary ...
Last updated 4/13/18 10:34:11 PM PDT

	Ordered product sales	Units
Today	$10,649.92	77
7 Days	$29,476.81	495
15 Days	$46,234.93	1,038
30 Days	$71,050.53	2,032

View more of your sales statistics

These numbers will show you how much potential your business can have with Amazon.

Be Patient & Build Your Amazon Business

If you are starting, do not launch ALL your product ideas on Amazon. Do your research and focus on a few products at a time. This will give you a chance to learn how Amazon works and gradually optimize. Managing too many listings when you first start off will be overwhelming and will leave a bad imprint on your Amazon account since some of your listings will not be fully optimized, and bad reviews can make a significant impact (start slow and be patient).

When someone first starts selling on Amazon, their product(s) do poorly because of no experience. They always think of giving up and think it is not worth it. Eventually, most of the clients we work with, after a few trial and errors, changing keywords, listing optimizations, etc., finally start hitting their targets. The more you sell, the more opportunities you have to make mistakes and learn from them. At first, sell a few items, then branch out, set goals, and work your way towards them.

Just to reiterate what we've touched on so far, Amazon spams you with tons of new things to do for your business. At first, stick to the basics and don't try to do everything at once. Amazon will push very hard for you to fulfill with them. However, if you have the right product(s) and want to pay the charge for FBA, then do it. My recommendation is to start without the FBA tag and familiarize yourself with the Amazon Marketplace. Follow your intuition and only turn to FBA when you're ready.

What Are Your Competitors Doing?

If you choose a product that falls into a highly competitive niche, then there are a few things that you should be considering. These are the things you should think about before entering a competitive market:

- *Does my product or service solve a specific problem for a specific set of people?*
- *What are the startup costs associated with this business (inventory cost & shipping cost)?*
- *How long will my goals take to be achieved?*
- *How competitive is the market?*

- *How can I differentiate my product(s) in this pre-existing market?*
- *How is the competition getting sales?*

These questions will allow you to contemplate on your decisions and help you tackle tasks that need to be completed. The most important thing is 'to never get ahead of yourself' and situate one task at a time.

When you check the competition, do a quick search on Amazon and see who the top dogs are in that niche; see what they do and what works for them. If your competition has around 100 reviews and you know they generate a good amount of sales, you have struck gold. Some listings may even have a couple hundred more, which would be a close second place but could be a bit more competitive. Certain listings have 1000+ reviews. The chances are that niche has a plethora of listings trying to fight for that nice chunk of sales. We recommend you go to battle with those listings a bit later in your e-commerce profession.

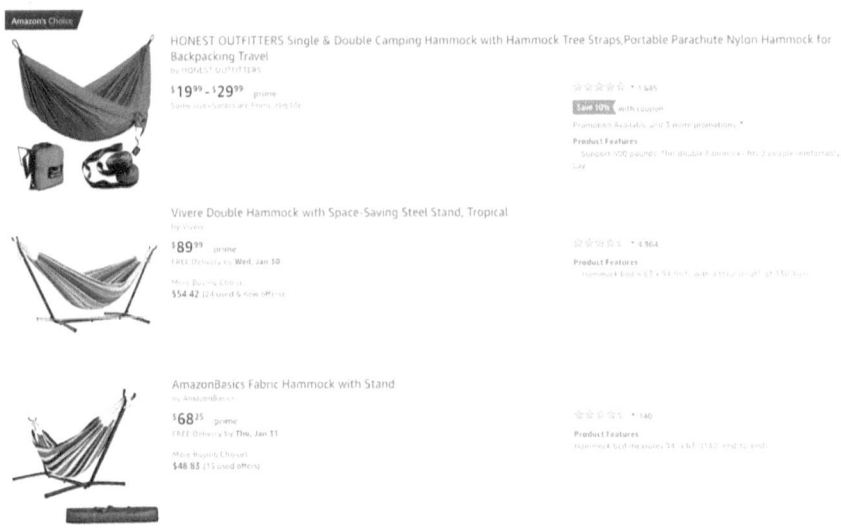

The three key components of differentiating yourself among countless listings are Title, Price, and Reviews.

The rule of thumb is that the number of reviews on a listing typically shows how much competition you are dealing with. Remember that if you do end up settling on the product, it takes a good amount of patience, hard work, and a vast amount of research to match or surpass what your competitors have been doing.

Time, effort, and trials and errors need to be accumulated to succeed on Amazon or any e-commerce marketplace. The best product to settle on would be one that has a high demand and low competition. There are tools like *JungleScout* and *Sellics* that can help you decipher what your product will be, or hire an agency to do all the hard work.

07

SOCIAL MEDIA ADVERTISING VS. GOOGLE ADS

"Your top of the funnel content must be intellectually divorced from your product but emotionally wed to it."
- Joe Chernov

Times are changing rapidly, and the most prominent tactics of promoting your business are evolving. In this chapter, we'll discuss the pros and cons of using social media and Google Ads and how they both could impact your business goals.

The definition of our topics here:

- *Google Ads*: Google Ads is Google's online advertising program. Through these ads, you can create online ads to reach people exactly when they're interested in the products and services that you offer.
- *Social Media Advertising*: The practice of advertising through platforms such as Instagram, Facebook, Twitter, Tumbler, Pinterest, etc., using text and/or visuals to promote a certain service or product.

ADVANTAGES OF USING SOCIAL MEDIA ADVERTISING

Social Media Is One of the Fastest Ways to Spread the Word

If you have a big fan base or are growing one, you can tweet, post on Facebook or Instagram, and your message can instantly go to thousands of users around the world. Many people using phones to know how addictive they are, and one of the reasons is because of social media. Taking advantage of this will be a great benefit to your business.

It's Good for SEO Traffic

Signs are showing that social media is being used to help for ranking purposes by both Google and Bing. Making posts on your social media accounts will relay traffic from your social platforms to your website; this will tell Google and Bing that your site is a leading factor in user searches.

Most Social Media Platforms Are a Growing Trend

Social media is a trend you cannot ignore if you want to stay close to your customers and in sync with the latest developments in marketing. Social platforms are the key to building a B2C (business-to-consumer) relationship that has never been experienced in any era until now.

The Ultimate Business to Customer Relationship

With social media, your customers can show that they like a product or piece of content by commenting and sharing (like the tweet, +1, etc.). By using this information, you can gauge what content to keep on creating for your audience.

WHY COMPANIES ARE HESITANT TO START
SOCIAL MEDIA ADVERTISING

Time and Money Investment

A small business can usually get by with a person combining social media posting responsibilities with other duties.

However, when your business starts to grow, hiring a person or agency to manage your social media and communications becomes increasingly necessary. Using social media effectively is a full-time job, with creating content, targeting audiences, creating ad campaigns, increasing engagement, and more. These tasks need to be monitored by a designated Social Media Manager or team.

Reputation Management

One of the reasons why you are on social media in the first place is to enhance your reputation. Using social media is a perfect way to increase your reputation because of the accessible avenues and rapid pace your content can be shared. This can backfire. One wrong comment or an offensive post can lead to a dent on your reputation, which can take an extended amount of time to mend.

Harmful Customer Reviews

Social media is also a big platform for customers to complain about your products and services. Not everyone will directly contact you for any issues; they may land on your company's social media profiles and post complaints or negative feedback/reviews about your content. The more claims you get, the more your brand will experience hardship. Managing and responding to reviews and giving grieving customers a solution is a key to managing this platform.

Difficult to Measure Certain Social Media Results

The only platforms that allow you to view your engagement endeavors entirely are Instagram and Facebook; other platforms such as LinkedIn, Twitter, etc., have minimal means to measure your actions. All other platforms can be measured, of course. However, it takes quite an amount of time to gather that information.

Research your market and find out where they are looking.

ADVANTAGES OF USING GOOGLE ADS

Creating a Google Ads Campaign Can Be Quick

You can be up and running on Google Ads in a concise amount of time. While there is a lot more to Google Ads as a whole than just campaigns, ad groups, keywords, and ads. Do a bit of keyword research, decide a budget plan, set up a campaign, and a few relevant ad groups, make a couple of ads, and that is it. Your ads will appear as soon as they've been approved, which usually is instantaneous.

Huge Chance of Exposure

You have the chance to appear on the first page of the internet's largest search engine. That alone should be a huge factor in budgeting Google Ads into your marketing plan; that is a tremendous amount of exposure! Your business is appearing to someone who's actively searching for what you offer when they need it. Which is a perfect opportunity to showcase a summary of what your business has to contribute to the potential customer?

You Have Full Control of Your Ads

You can turn your campaigns on/off with just a click. You can even have control of what ad groups or keywords you want to have paused. This is a huge advantage that search engine advertising has over social media advertising.

Even though social media advertising is still relativity in its infancy phase compared to Google Ads, paid social advertising is slowly evolving into a similar approach to paid search advertising. If you want to reach the most amount of people in the shortest amount of time, Google Ads is the way to go.

Simple Analytic Tools

When it comes to Google Ads, Google does a great job of measuring your work. Whether using applications such as Google Analytics, Google AdSense, or Google Tag Manager, these can all help give a detailed report on what you are working with.

Keyword research takes a long time, come up with 25-50 keywords that your audience searches for.

DISADVANTAGES OF USING GOOGLE ADS

You Pay for Each Click to Your Website

This means that you pay whenever someone clicks on your ad, regardless of whether that click converted or not. So you may get clicks from visitors who have no intention of ever buying your product or service. This can be a bit costly if you do not know what you are doing, and your campaign is not designed to target the right audience.

Competitive Industries Have Higher Cost-Per-Clicks

If your competitors are already using Google Ads, this might be the reason why you want to start your campaign. However, the competition can be intimidating, and as a result, the cost-per-click will be much higher than anticipated. If your keyword bid is too low, then your ads could be relegated to page 2 or 3 of the search results.

Unfortunately, this is a pay-to-play field, and to get the best results, you normally need a high bid. On the bright side, bidding is much more affordable on social media. This is a nice alternative or supplementary route to run on top of your Google Ads.

Time-Consuming to Learn Keyword Targeting

You need to ensure that you have added sufficient negative keywords to your campaigns or your ads could be shown to the wrong users. Another time-consuming task is getting all the right keywords to target the right people effectively. This is an ongoing process as well; each week, you will monitor what users are searching for and adjust your negative keywords and primary keywords accordingly.

WRAPPING UP THE SOCIAL MEDIA &
GOOGLE ADS DEBATE

It doesn't matter what platform you end up using for your business to expand as we've stated before; it's all trial and error. Depending on your business and the market it serves, each platform has its pros and cons. Do not be afraid to try some platforms you have never used before. You never know, one of them could be a ticket to another flight your business can take off on.

Master 2-3 avenues to gain a new audience and work your way up from there. Never limit yourself to one platform.

08

WHAT A

SOCIAL MEDIA

MANAGER

REALLY DOES

FOR

BUSINESS

"Good brands reflect the histories of the time and the group of people that made them. They cannot be copied. They cannot be recycled."
- Richard Branson

As you already know, the digital marketing space is evolving at a rapid pace, and chasing right behind it is you and your business. It can be a daunting task to try to juggle your business goals and your marketing goals.

These two objectives should be focused on 100%, and even a little slip of pondering your next decision for your organization can leave you behind your competitors, and we do not want that.

"Good companies will meet needs; great companies will create markets."
- Philip Kotler

Philip Kotler is an amazing marketer, and we have seen his speeches numerous times. As everyone in the business world, we all know businesses are like a living thing, always changing. If a business cannot keep up with the times, it will gradually rot away and become extinct. Sometimes it is a little too late for the organization to withstand the effects of change. Successful businesses, for instance, Blockbuster, Toys"R"Us, Pets.com, Compaq, General Motors, and Nokia are all substantial examples of what change can do to a company.

Digital Media Marketing, Digital Advertising, Social Media Marketing, Digital Marketing, and even SEO marketing have one goal in common: to get your business seen by the right audience at the right time and ultimately land that lead or sale. This is where visibility on Instagram, Facebook, Google, Bing, and Amazon comes into play. These platforms are paramount to your success and ensuring the longevity of your organization and goals.

What Is a Social Media Manager?

A Social Media Manager is primarily responsible for the management and marketing duties of specific media platforms like Instagram, Facebook, Yelp, LinkedIn, Twitter, Snapchat, etc. These channels will be the focal point for a Social Media Manager's duties. Some of these tasks are:

- Administrate the creation and publishing of relevant, original, high-quality content for your organization.
- Identify and improve organizational development aspects that would improve content creation (employee group activities, recognition, and rewards for participation in company endeavors and online review building).
- Create a regular publishing schedule for social media platforms.
- Leverage the right analytical tools to manage and grow your media presence.
- Implement a content editorial calendar to manage content and plan specific, timely marketing campaigns.
- Target specific audiences with agency techniques.

Clear Business Objectives

Why do customers or clients come to your business? Why do they pick your company over a competitor's? Does your organization have a social consciousness? When you get the answers to these questions, your company will reach new heights with customer connections. When you connect to the public, you are essentially connecting to potential customers. Having a social presence and allowing your Social Media Manager to help your company achieve a social existence will significantly enhance the reputation of your company and will guarantee customers in the long run.

An excellent "why buy here" message is unique to your company. It has to be backed up by facts (awards, numbers, in-store policies) and answer questions such as "What's in it for me?" Your potential customer or client should know these answers; these are extremely important and could be deciding factors. Using outlets like Instagram and Facebook could be a perfect opportunity to let your potential audience find out these answers before a transaction.

Social media is a perfect way to get your business message across and give a "why here?" to your audience.

Identifying & Targeting Your Audience

The service or product your business is offering is not for everyone. Until you accept the notion that you need to focalize on the product at hand and keep your market focus on the right areas, you'll constrict your business's ability to grow where you would like it to be.

Writing down some key points about your best clients can help attract more like-minded individuals. Having information on their behaviors, attributes, and wants can give you a leg up in this social media world. Teaming up with your Social Media Manager, sharing these insights, and reaching out to said clients can help in the succession of your business.

Once you know more about your target audience, you can use data to proclaim your message. Facebook is invaluable for exploring audiences that are interested in your product or service and can narrow down your exact audience. It can be quite fascinating and also a bit scary. Being a marketing company that specializes in this, we cannot stress the importance of social media advertising enough. If your manager (or you) does not understand your goals, you need to find another one.

Engagement Strategies to Help Your Business

Your Social Media Manager should listen, respond, ask questions, and engage with your audience. There should be a practiced approach on how he/she responds to organic (non-paid) leads that appear in the comment section of your posts. People will ask questions and sometimes want to engage in a sale. The Social Media Manager should have knowledge and experience of your sales process to respond appropriately. If your manager does not know how to respond, they should direct the lead to the appropriate person or group within your business.

If a lead asks a question, your manager should answer it and follow it up with a question back to engage them further, eventually guiding them to a product display page, signup form, or appointment.

Leverage Facebook and Instagram Ads to promote your content and increase your audience reach, and as your page content grows, your following will grow with the right manager. This will inevitability get your content seen more often in newsfeeds, and you'll find it easier to engage fans/followers and build those relationships.

Making these connections through social media channels as a business can play a huge role in a potential transaction. They may not buy that product you're selling or what service you are providing just yet. However, in due time, your organization's name may pop up in their mind and watch who they turn to for that transaction or refer a friend or family member to your organization.

Having your Social Media Manager engage with your growing audience will build your company's reputation as socially aware. Including an advocate to build relationships on these social media platforms gives your organization a beneficial pedestal among many companies already implementing these practices (some examples: *Google, Ben & Jerry's, LEGO, Warby Parker, IBM, Zappos, Apple, Starbucks* and many more).

If your Social Media Manager knows how to deliver your content with stunning visuals and emotionally grabbing words, you have a winner!

Using the Right Social Media Platforms With the Right Conversion Strategy

With growth and engagement strategies in place, the Social Media Manager's job is to convert fans into customers, and your marketing plan should outline the steps required.

The more advanced forms of Facebook marketing utilize Facebook ads, custom audiences, and compelling landing pages. Be sure to include a call to action and a lead form on your landing page to ensure your lead has a path to purchase (and your Social Media Manager has a way to follow up). For example, using Instagram and Facebook can bring many potential clients and customers that want to view what you are offering. Our research shows that it takes an average of three visits/interactions for a client to make an initial purchase. Keep this in mind for your marketing endeavors.

If you have a product you would like to sell, and the only channel for your audience to view your catalog is on your site, a great alternative to place your inventory would be on the Amazon Marketplace. This is an ideal strategy to use for physical products or even services to funnel your social media audience to your website or Amazon storefront.

I've found most companies need advice and support with conversion strategy. Find yourself a well-driven company to point you in the right direction, and it will pay off in the long run. Digital Marketing is an ever-growing field, and so is your business. Do your organization a favor and build a social sphere to ensure your business will be cemented in numerous timelines on this Earth.

Figuring out which platform your business can utilize is stressful and time-consuming, find out which one is good for you and work your way from there!

09

HIRING THE

RIGHT SOCIAL

MEDIA

MANAGER

"Content is king, but marketing is queen, and runs the household."
-Gary Vaynerchuk

There are a plethora of Social Media Managers out there, and the supply and demand are growing at an outstanding rate. People have noticed the impact social media (especially Instagram) can have for their companies.

Whether it is showing off your business, distributing knowledge, sending a message, creating a movement, establishing a presence, whatever it is you seek to accomplish along these lines, it can be met on Instagram.

This is why if you are an organization or someone that does not know social media from the inside out, hiring a manager will give you the upper hand. If you do need one or want tips regarding social media tactics and managers in general, this chapter will benefit you!

Does Your Social Media Manager Understand Your Brand or Goal?

Your Social Media Manager's job becomes much easier when you've effectively-outlined your identity or goal to them.

It's crucial for Social Media Managers to go over your ambitions for the future, what direction you want your company to go, and to have a similar mindset as your own.

Hiring the right manager or agency can help your social media advertising efforts, meaning they will engage the right users on the designated platform(s) so that your brand will expand with word of mouth or advertising with targeted ads.

Creating the best-targeted advertisement will maximize the Return on Investment (ROI) and make you and your Social Media Manager happy.

Businesspeople often think it is a fast road to building a brand on a social platform; that belief is sadly internally false. Building a social presence on any platform is like a seed, slowly turning into a sapling and then a beautiful tree. Make sure you have the patience and the perfect person or people to help you nurture your brand.

The patience will be rewarding.

THE TWO MOST IMPORTANT SOCIAL
MEDIA METRICS TO BE TRACKED

Engagement is number one. Whichever channel you are planning to use, there needs to be a measurable conversation around your brand. The content that is put out to your audience is one of the key ingredients for a recipe for a great engagement.

If you do not create the right content, expect to see minimal results. Your Social Media Manager should excel in capturing your potential clientele/audience with witty sentences and captivating expressions.

Leads are number two. What's their track record with Instagram Ads? LinkedIn Ads? Have they run a successful social campaign that created leads? Ask them what their approach is, and if you agree with that approach (and make sure you have an open mind and give their practices a try), chances are they will be willing to meet halfway.

It is vital for your social media's keeper to have a fast response rate for your leads. Listening and responding to inquiries promptly will show that you are willing to accommodate at any time. The customer is always a priority. Dig deep into how your overseer is for your social accounts and see if they are the right fit.

Each social platform has its analytics for you to track;
get familiar with them.

Do They Have a Blog About Their Knowledge?

If your candidate is an agency, ask about the content they are creating and if they are active bloggers. Additionally, ask to view their relevant blogs to show you what you are getting into and to give you better insight into their knowledge of the subject at hand.

Blogs not only show their knowledge, but they also show that they have an active following that enjoys what they produce. If your potential account manager does not have any blogs, consider that a red flag.

It's vital that your candidate has an understanding of how content drives everything in digital marketing, such as Search Engine Optimization (SEO), social media, blogging, and search engine platforms like Google and Bing.

This will put you in the right spot to succeed and will give you the best Return on Investment (ROI). A working understanding of platforms that create websites is also a plus.

How Experienced Are They on Social Media?

Yes, experience matters, it always has. You do not want someone fresh out of high school, fiddling with your campaign budget or trying to target the audience for their objective. You want to hire someone with experience. The only thing is that finding someone with 10+ years of experience will be nearly impossible to accomplish unless they have been around since the Myspace boom and were promoting their content on there.

Even then, most social media platforms are in a league of their own and are not to be taken lightly. So bear in mind the age of a platform because most of these social platforms are no more than 5-10 years old.

Smaller companies can efficiently utilize 1-3 years of SMM (Social Media Management) experience. A larger company with high levels of online traffic and responsibility will probably want to hire someone with 3-5 years of experience.

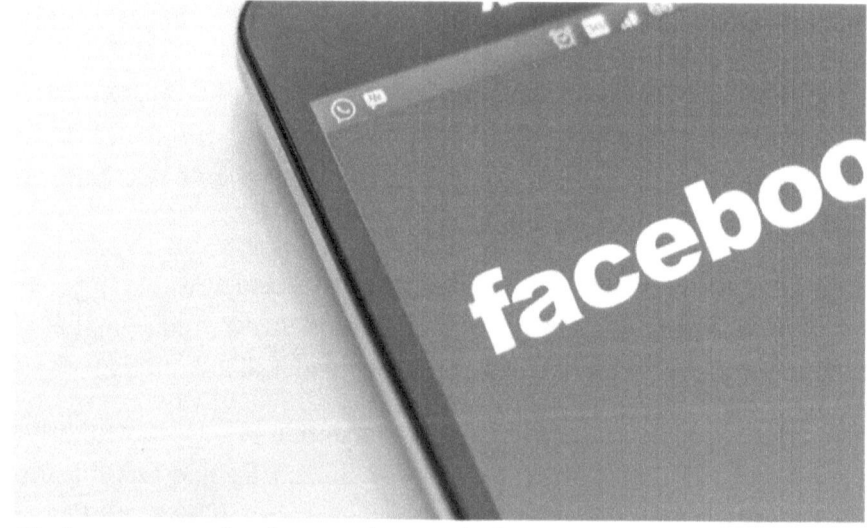

Find a manager that knows the trends for each platform. Have some questions ready when you speak to your potential manager.

What You Need to Know

These key questions need to be answered for you to find the right candidate for your business. Having the right social media management to oversee your marketing efforts on your social media platform(s) will give you a huge leg over the competition. Allowing your audience to follow your movements and showing them that you have a story will allow you to have a better connection with them even before making the transaction you are seeking.

Do your research about who you pick and take your time in doing so. Trust your gut! Leverage all the platforms you can get your hands on; this will only make your business grow. Sometimes it even takes a couple of tries to find the right partner for your company. One of our clients had to go through four agencies to find us. Every agency has a different mindset than another. Pick the best, with the right cost.

10

PROVEN WAYS TO

GET FREE

ADVERTISING FOR

ANY BUSINESS

"If you're trying to persuade people to do something, or buy something, it seems to me you should use their language, the language they use every day, the language in which they think."
- David Ogilvy

Many business owners may become frustrated with their advertising tactics as the budget can often limit the number of people reached with their ads. Most of these individuals, unfortunately, are on the brink of giving up or just trying to find new ways to advertise without breaking the bank.

So, is it possible to advertise for free?

Of course!

There are numerous amounts of free business advertising routes online today that allow businesses to get more out of their budgets. These open channels supplement paid advertising to improve brand awareness, increase leads, and boost conversions. When you include some of these proven tactics in your digital marketing strategy, you can drastically cut down on advertising costs. Plus, who does not like FREE things, especially when they can completely change your business trajectory?

Here we'll talk about a few options for your digital marketing efforts that you will have at your disposal that are entirely free. We love to see your work thrive (especially up and coming businesses). Take advantage of this chapter and the vast amounts of information on the internet to boost your business endeavors!

1. Blogging

Of course, this would be the first free advertising tactic you can use for your business! Posting content on a business Blog, or any blog for that matter, is a great digital marketing strategy that can be 100% free to utilize. Sites like Wix and Blogger will allow you to get started with a blog completely free. You can set up your blog and start posting content instantly.

Tip: Make sure you have a great site for your visitors to browse while they read your blog posts!

For a small fee, you can set up a blog with your custom domain; we recommend doing this as it helps you build your brand and gives you a place to drive traffic. This will be a huge factor if you plan on doing this in the long run. If you already have a website, you can add a blog section to your current site where you will publish new blog posts for your leads and visitors to read.

Now comes the hard part; it's time to start creating content for your blog. For the best results, you'll want to publish content consistently. The more often you publish new posts, the better results you will get, which will be general business traffic and Search Engine Optimization (SEO).

Not sure where to begin? Can't find a topic to write about? Well, we have the perfect (free) solution for this. Check out this site called BuzzSumo. This site is being used by industry-leading businesses, and it is free! Just do some brainstorming and see what your target audience would enjoy; type in some topics using BuzzSumo, and you will be writing in no time!

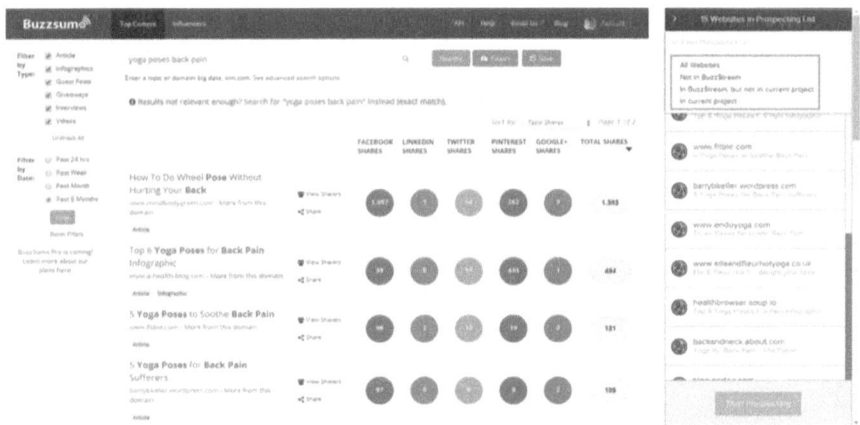

Find the topic your industry is about and become an expert at it. Write as many informative and giving articles as you can; your audience will thank you for it.

2. Create a "Google My Business" Page to Optimize for Local Search

One of the best ways to get free advertising is by claiming and working on your Google My Business (GMB) page. GMB listings are a free business listing tool that helps you improve visibility on Google Search and Google Maps within your area of business. If you run a business that requires your customers or clients to visit your facility, claiming your GMB page is a requirement to build additional searches and awareness.

Google My Business is a (proven) first step taken by thousands of businesses that want improvement on their reach online within the local market audience. By optimizing your GMB listing and making sure that all of your information is complete, you can help improve your rankings for local search results. Even if you do not have a brick-and-mortar type of facility, it is still paramount that you make a Google My Business page. This will provide better brand authority for your industry and give an added layer of authenticity.

Here's an example of what a GMB listing looks like on the search engine:

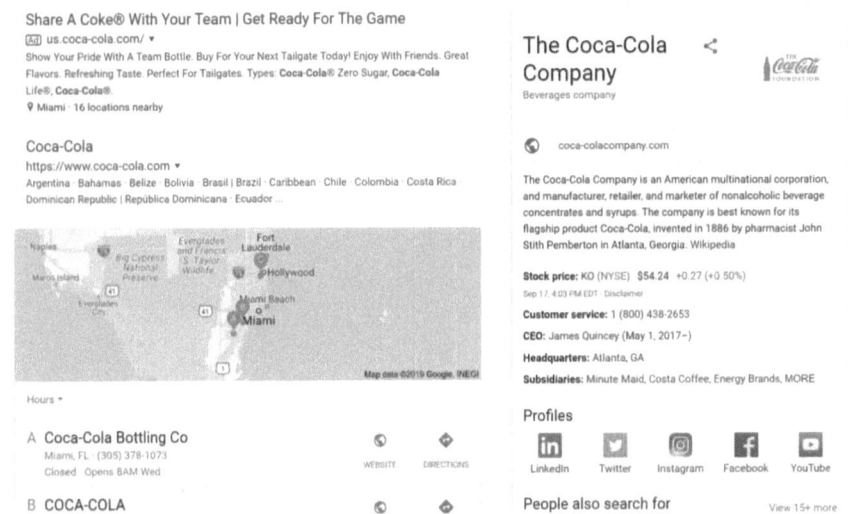

Coca-Cola makes sure they fully utilize GMB to
showcase their business.

3. Add Your Business on Yelp & Other Review Sites

Similar to Google My Business, Yelp can be a great avenue for free
advertising. You want to be in as many places as possible to improve
your online visibility and increase your reach. With this being said, you
need to look for other opportunities to include your business information
on online platforms, especially trusted and recognized online entities.

If you are not familiar with Yelp, it is an online review site that consumers use to get recommendations on everything from restaurants to bar-
bershops. Your customers can go on Yelp to leave your business a star-
rating and written review that other users can see when they look up
your business.

Using this free advertising route can be a perfect way to establish cred-
ibility among your local competition. Do not be fooled into Yelp being
solely for local business searches. How many times have you caught
yourself searching for places to go or places to eat when you are researching on Yelp?

There is a variety of other business listing sites that help you build a profile or registering for your business for free. Some globally recognized listing sites that you should look into include: Better Business Bureau(not free), Yellow Pages, and FourSquare. You could also consider industry-specific sites like Angie's List, Thumbtack, or TripAdvisor. Your business will be the deciding factor of where you would like your business information posted.

We recommend putting your details and all relevant business information in as many authoritative sites as you can.

Remember putting your business on some of these sites can have pros and cons, and one of the cons can be someone giving you a bad review. So make sure your customer service is sharp, and you meet the needs of all your inquiries. Consumers may come to your listing from the search engine or another person who has referred them. For this reason, you must keep these listings optimized regularly and incentivize your customers to leave positive reviews to increase your overall standing in the current marketplace. This will greatly differentiate you against the competition.

4. Answer Quora Questions

Another great free way to increase your business exposure online is by answering questions on Quora. Quora has been around for a reasonable amount of time, and it is primarily known for its Q&A feature; it allows users to ask questions and get answers from other users. Many industry-leading experts will use Quora to offer their insights and interact with high-quality potential leads while establishing themselves as an expert in their market.

This platform is an excellent place for businesses to demonstrate their knowledge and tap into another audience. Let's give you an example. Let's say you have an online boutique business. You might go on Quora to answer questions like "Where is the best place to buy a hat to use during the winter?" or "How do I choose the right shoes for my outfit?"

Answering relevant questions in your marketplace on Quora gives you another fantastic opportunity to provide value for your target audience. When you give a complete and descriptive answer to a Quora user's question, you are not only educating a prospective customer, you're also getting your name and your business name recognized in areas that your target customers might look for answers to their questions.

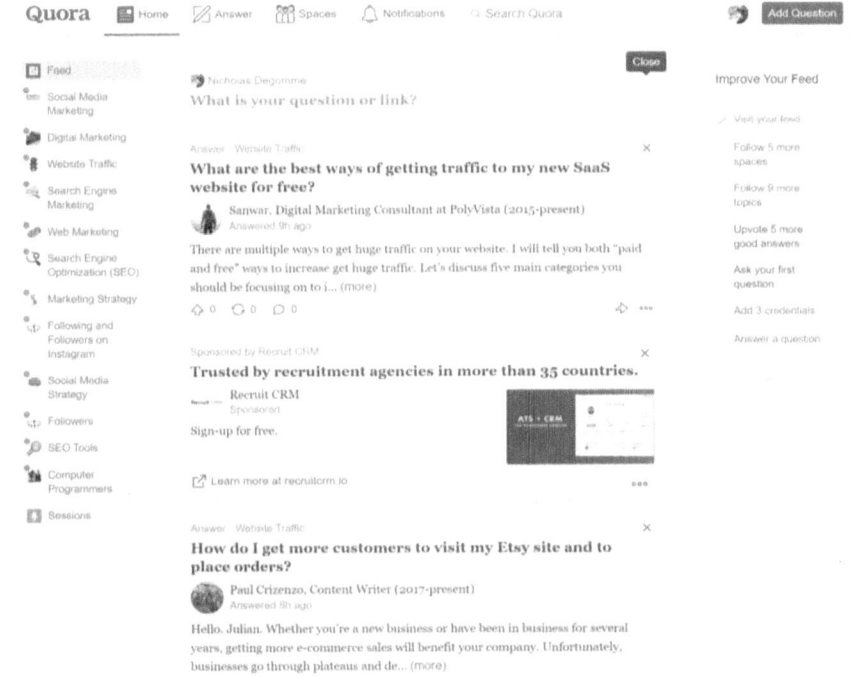

Answering the right questions in a precise manner will give you instant authority.

5. Advertise Your Business Using an Email Signature

This one is a hidden and not very talked-about way of subtly advertising your business. The tactic is using your email signature. This is a very non-invasive way to build awareness for your company. Even the non-marketing emails that you send to suppliers, colleagues, and prospects can be a great place to advertise your website and social profiles for free.

All you need to do is add links to your website, social profiles, or other business-related links,such as a featured blog post, to your email signature. Creating a professionally branded email signature is a perfect way to stand out in a potential client's inbox.

T.L. Smith
Owner, @AfterHoursVA
804-357-1163 | tsmith@AfterHoursVA.com |
www.AfterHoursVA.com

Latest Facebook Status I've been getting a lot of GNW through my listing on Thumbtack. Add your listing today for FREE. There is a small fee ($...   Read More

> Load up your email signature, but be careful not to put in too much irrelevant information.

Notice that the email signature above has the necessary contact information that is the industry norm, such as email, phone number, and address. However, this information is a direct link to the company website. Also, this business shows that it is very active in different social spaces by including a plethora of social icons. Again make sure whatever you put on your email signature will give positive advertising to your business.

5. Networking at an Event

Connecting with like-minded professionals at industry networking events is a great free advertising method. This is a perfect place where business can be spoken about, and new connections can be formed without being intrusive.

Make sure networking events you are targeting meet your business standards; this will ensure you are meeting high- qualified leads. For example, the "Miami Under 40 Networking Mixer" event will primarily be filled with participants who are interested in networking with high-caliber and well-established businesses.

Everyone was new to something once.

Speaking at a networking event about a topic related to your industry is another way to show off your expertise and your business. Giving a well-rounded, confident speech can boost brand awareness, as well as prove your business is qualified to solve industry challenges.

If you are not used to speaking to an audience or do not know what to talk about, brainstorm different topics, volunteer at various upcoming networking events, and trade association conventions. Doing this will build up confidence gradually. You might even look into starting your own podcast!

6. Social Media Advertising

We saved the best for last. Some may think, "But social media advertising is only effective using paid ads!" Thankfully not! Using social media can be a great way to advertise for free if you know what you are doing! Additionally, it's free to set up a social media account for your business, post relevant content, engage with users, and share your business ideas and solutions.

When you post content to your business's social media page, you are taking advantage of the opportunity to reach and start a conversation with your clientele or potential audience. Posting relevant content that targets specific groups of people will not only build awareness of your brand but additionally drive more traffic back to your website.

Create stunning content no one can ignore.

By posting questions or giving your followers something to think about, you can spark a conversation with your followers or browsing audience. Attentively responding to comments and answering questions is an excellent way of showing your audience that your brand cares about them and wants to help! Huge companies such as Coca- Cola, GM, and other powerhouses, are using this technique to their advantage, so why not start now?

Sure, they probably have a social media agency taking care of their social profiles and are dishing out an obscene amount of money. This does not hinder you or your business from hiring an affordable and reputable agency to manage your social media advertising and management efforts.

Start Your Free Business Advertising Efforts

Now that you know all the ways that you can take advantage of free business advertising online, it's time to get started. As you work to include these tactics in your digital marketing strategy, remember:

- Blogging is a perfect way to make connections with leads, and all it costs you is a bit of time. Some businesses even make money doing this!
- Use authoritative sites such as Yelp, Quora, Yellow-Pages, etc., to authenticate and build a well-established brand.
- Networking can establish great trust if you are a local business and want to improve word-of-mouth marketing.
- Social media is a free way to reach and engage with a new audience online.
- There are many other opportunities, such as guest blogging, that you can take advantage of to expand your reach online for free. Always search for new ways to advertise your business!

Though these tactics are free for your business advertising efforts, you will still need to dedicate time to making these free advertising methods work optimally for you. If your business can't afford the time to dedicate to these tactics, you can still accomplish this by partnering with a digital marketing agency.

CONCLUSION

"Amazing things will happen when you listen to the consumer."
- Jonathan Midenhall

A SHORT STORY

Social Media Marketing Revamped is a short and simple tool that will set up anyone wanting to learn about digital marketing and lead them down the right path. It is meant to be a gateway to those new and motivated or a refresher for those that are already familiar with this industry.

Finding a new social media platform that you have never ventured to is just the beginning of a new path for your business. Every outlet you expose your business to is another opportunity and a whole new audience.

However, each avenue you take when you start to advertise your company or yourself needs to have a well-thought-out plan and needs to be coupled with short and long-term goals. Sadly, many people fall just short of their goals and get discouraged about the results obtained.

For the readers that have been discouraged or have had a major setback as a business owner or influencer, here's a little snippet of my beginnings.

For many aspiring business owners, there is a turning point in which the individual gets drawn into actually being an owner and accumulating their own money. The money being earned is a result of their hard work and dedication to their ideas and their goals, which is what I felt when I decided to venture down this path.

Before owning a digital marketing agency, I was searching for new ways to bring in a new source of income. I started searching "How to make money" or "Making money with a job," and I came across selling on Amazon which (thankfully) at the time was a very enticing opportunity due to it being a way to gain money without interfering with my current job.

I pursued this opportunity and created an Amazon Seller Account. I started researching viable products to sell using different research platforms, haggled with Chinese manufacturers, and bought the product(s).

After 3 weeks on Amazon, I accumulated an astonishing ZERO sales.

After this deflating experience, I started researching ways to draw in more customers. Through trial and error, I learned what worked and what didn't (I even started advertising on Amazon itself). Finally, after a full month, I got my first sale! I was ecstatic until... I realized how much I invested in inventory and how much was spent on advertising. I was crushed.

There is a very pivotal point in our lives in which we can either give up and move on or persevere, knowing that if you keep pushing, your goals can be accomplished. That one sale was all I needed to know there is a market for what I was selling and which motivated me to push forward. I threw myself into researching successful people in this field and learned from their trials and tribulations.

Finally, after three whole months, I started seeing some traction. First, it was three or four sales a week, but eventually sales became so consistent that at this point there has not been a week where I haven't had a sale.

Many people will fall in love with that first sale feeling, knowing that there is a person in this world that needs what you have to offer. Whether what you offer is a service, a product, or a brand, all you need is that one person who is interested in igniting that drive. There is a market for what you are offering. If you are a restaurateur that is failing, it could be the location, cuisine, etc. If you are an influencer that is not having success, chances are it is the niche you have picked to draw your audience.

There is always a reason why you are not seeing the results you have been longing for. Sometimes it is a minor tweak that can change everything, and sometimes it takes time. Every instance is different, however it's up to you to hold onto that hope and push forward.

Thankfully, agencies like DEGOM Marketing strive to make digital marketing services affordable. Offering a bevy of result-oriented services to a diverse portfolio of corporate clients. DEGOM Marketing is a digital marketing company that specializes in social media and search engine platforms with a constant focus on lead generation and sales. We position our clients for success through social media management services, social media marketing services, Google Ads, Microsoft Ads, web design, and premium consulting.

I hope this book serves you well, and you have learned more than what you knew before reading Social Media Marketing Revamped. Set your goals high and always be willing to learn new techniques to better not only your business but yourself!

SOCIAL MEDIA MARKETING REVAMPED

ABOUT THE AUTHOR

Nicholas is a digital marketing expert from Miami, Florida that specializes in social media and search engine platforms with a constant focus on lead generation and sales. His company DEGOM Marketing positions clients for success through social media management services, social media marketing services, search engine marketing, Amazon advertising and optimization, web design & offers lead driven consulting. Nicholas is also the author of *Social Media Marketing Revamped.* A short novel that describes the current digital marketing trends and tactics. His novel demonstrates how he uses his proven tactics for his successful clientele. Nicholas created this book for any type of business or person that needs insight into starting a digital marketing strategy.

Any Feedback or Questions?

Email me at nick@degomglobalmarketing.com or contact me via our website or the following social networks:

Website: www.degomglobalmarketing.com

Facebook: www.facebook.com/degom.marketing/

Instagram: www.instagram.com/degom.marketing/

LinkedIn: www.linkedin.com/degom-marketing/

Pinterest: www.pinterest.com/degom_marketing/

DID YOU ENJOY SOCIAL MEDIA

MARKETING REVAMPED?

If you found this book helpful and believe it is worth sharing, please do so! It will help anyone interested in the digital marketing industry and will help me tremendously.

In addition, if you have a few moments now to leave a short review where ever you received this book, I will be extremely grateful.

All the best, and thank you so much for reading *Social Media Marketing Revamped*.

Nick.

www.ingramcontent.com/pod-product-compliance
Lightning Source LLC
Chambersburg PA
CBHW030951240526
45463CB00016B/2337